"Not R Spiritual!

A Holistic Journey Beyond Time and Space

Essay #1

CRISTI-ANA MONTESANTO

A SPECIAL NOTE

Dear Reader,

This is self-published material.
I was involved in all preparations every step of the way.
I had lots of help from competent people.
In spite of all our efforts, we assume that you will find imperfections of all sorts.
We apologize for any inconvenience.

If you find any imperfections and would like to let us know, please contact us at:
https://cristi-anamontesanto.com/contact/

As to my style… Well, what can I say? It is all mine!
No apologies necessary here.

With all my light,
Cristi-Ana

DEDICATION

I dedicate this Essay #1 to everybody on their spiritual path who consciously wish to harness the connection to their soul.

May you find many treasures and may you cherish them forever!

TABLE OF CONTENTS

ACKNOWLEDGEMENTS

This is no "typical" or "traditional" list.
It cannot be.
I always go beyond the human level when meeting someone. I prefer to also connect to their soul.
There are so very many people I am grateful to, but instead of mentioning any names I take this opportunity to give my thanks to their souls.
I cannot express how lucky I feel for the many wonderful and joyful encounters. I am touched by our interactions both on the human and the spiritual levels.

Last but not least, I thank my own soul for the power, the light, the wisdom, the happiness and the guidance I have always received.
I don't remember in which incarnation I transcended the state of separation between my human personality and my soul, but I do know I started experiencing wholeness many lifetimes ago.
I regard the connection to my soul as the only foundation for my life. Everything else follows.

I would like to invite all human beings harnessing the connection to their souls to join us who are already connected and celebrate with us!
Let us all be consciously whole!

With lots of laughter for all of us,
Cristi-Ana

1 THE BEGINNING OF THE BEGINNING

Even though I know it is not true, I have moments when I feel as if I am the only person on the entire planet who experiences spiritual pain.. From all possible aspects of pain, spiritual pain is the most intense in my case. I do not need to know on the personal level any human being in pain in order to experience a massive negative reaction in my heart chakra, in connection with all my etheric chakras. My awareness on the impersonal level is so sharp that I am catapulted out of normal human consciousness, to find myself in the middle of my soul fully alive and fully attuned to the miracle of creation and the disparity of its manifestation on the physical plane.

I assume neither I, nor all the others like me would have experienced any spiritual pain, had creation been on the physical plane the way it was intended to be. I regard that original state as consisting of the following elements: harmony, joy, effortlessness, awareness, peace, balance, transcendence, insight, intelligence, prosperity, and success. The question has bothered me endlessly: "What went wrong?" and more than that, "Why cannot humanity manage to implement or restore the original state?" I know we are coming from the same source, we are all going back to the same source, and in between the only thing that differentiates us is our level of consciousness.

Religiosity does not qualify for a meaningful level of consciousness. It represents the most obvious aspect of the fact that the manifestation of creation went wrong, and I am saying that because religiosity is based on the three pillars of fear, denial, and punishment - which are all in contradiction with that original state, made up of completely different elements, as mentioned above. I respect the human desire to stay connected to the source of creation and I regard our state of connection to divinity as the only natural state. It is just that fear, denial, and punishment are creating a separation from our natural connection to the universe.

The most absurd phenomenon is thinking that we humans have to go to war in god's name. Humans only show their deep misunderstandings when they display arrogant insights. Why would we ever think that god needs something from us? And if we are so arrogant to believe that he needs something from us, why the hell did we not agree on harmony, joy, effortlessness, awareness, peace, balance, transcendence, insight, intelligence, prosperity, and success?

My spiritual journey does not start on the physical plane, but for the time being it is easier to communicate experiences as a human being.

2 ROMANIA DURING COMMUNISM

Being born under the Communist regime is a most unfortunate event by any standard. Beyond the violation of human rights of the most basic kind - such as not being allowed to travel, not being allowed to express any criticism, not being allowed to think, feel and act freely - Communism has the infamous function of undermining human decency, human value, and especially human spirit. The system had no transparency and no accountability, it was dysfunctional on many levels and there was a high probability that sooner or later people would experience a bump with psychopathology, especially paranoia.

Paradoxically, Communism as I experienced it in Romania at the time of my childhood, being as perverse as it was, managed to enable a detour from the basic mis-manifestation of creation: religion. By denying the existence of god, Communism provided an unexpected escape from the familiar pitfall. I grew up free from the idea of divinity and fear, denial, and punishment. It is hard to believe that a political system which is externally extremely oppressive, would manage to offer, regarding religion, the internal freedom that cannot be found in non-Communist systems. I suppose it is due to the law of polarity that even the most negative can create a positive.

3 THE ROMANIAN ORTHODOX CHURCH

To continue our double-bind with Communism and its denial of religion, let me take you to the realm of the schizophrenic marriage between godlessness and un-freedom. Although god did not exist officially, I never observed a Romanian miss the involvement of the church when it came to baptisms, weddings and burials. The church was indeed a marginalized experience, reduced to a symbolic act void of any specific message, except the unofficial acknowledgment that centuries of human tradition cannot be erased from one day to the next even by the most inhumane political dogma.

I have to confess that Communism is about godlessness and that Communism is not about godlessness. This statement is not meant to cause confusion. It only has the purpose of indicating a lack of congruence in the human experience. You might think of the following analogy: when you have a fever you might take an aspirin, but when you don't have a fever you don't think of aspirin at all. It is not good to have to take aspirin, but you allow it its legitimate raison d'être. While aspirin might not cause a high degree of ambivalence in the normal person, Communism and its position to religion was an unintended side effect of denying the natural state between a human being and divinity. And what was my personal advantage of this denial? Divinity for me has nothing to do with the traditional views or attitudes which are called "normal" for religious people.

While my two parents baptized me at birth just like any normal people did, when I became a mother in the free world, I decided not to have my baby baptized. In the next few years I could become a grandmother and I plan to stay out of taking any sides pro or contra baptism regarding my grandchildren. When I was married I only went through the civil ceremony and I am at peace with that decision. I suppose if I regarded us humans as holy, I might also regard what we do as holy, marriage or otherwise, but since we are perfect imperfections it is best to humbly give up the "holy" for the plain "only human". I personally do not think that we are even getting close to practicing getting married as an act of spirituality simply because our consciousness does not yet display the elements of spirituality. In the case of my burial, I prefer no religious ceremony either. But I was not asked as a baby if I wanted to be baptized, and only god knows what they will do to me once I am dead. But since I will be out of the human sphere, I make the conscious choice not to let it bother me.

4 GYPSIES: AND I EVEN MANAGED TO LOVE THEM

Note:
I am aware that the term "Gypsies" is old-fashioned and nowadays associated with many prejudices. I know that after the fall of the Iron Curtain the world started talking about the Sintis and Romas, unfortunately I am not able to identify this minority in Romania either as the one or the other, because at the time of my childhood everybody knew them only as "Gypsies". I am not about terminology be it old or new, I am though, about human relationships beyond terminology. There is one more idea I would like to explain here. I am highly critical of getting involved in situations after the worst is over, instead of being active in the right place at the right time. My Gypsies would have needed help during Communism. Well? Nobody nationally or internationally bothered to intervene. Sticking to fixations on words is simply unspiritual. Maybe scientific, but unspiritual. I mean none of the negative connotations when I use the term "Gypsies".

7

Just like every totalitarian political system, Communism had many brainwashing techniques for us and one of them triggered our prejudice against the Gypsies. But lucky me, Ceausescu never knew my grandmother. She was the one who, intentionally or unintentionally, taught me some extremely valuable lessons about life. Ana did not bother with political systems. She had two household aides. And guess what? Irina and Stan were Gypsies. I grew up with them and I unconsciously internalized their kind and loving way towards me and my brother. For me it was always a pleasure to see them when I visited Mama Ana. When Irina and Stan babysat for us, we used to laugh a lot and I always felt sorry when they had to go. Of course, as a little girl I had no idea about minorities and/or race. You might think for a three or four-year-old girl that is OK. But I continued having difficulties understanding this type of prejudice even when I was ten and watched for the very first time the movie *Guess Who's Coming to Dinner*. I loved Spencer Tracy and Katharine Hepburn, but I never understood why a young white woman should not have married her young Black boyfriend. I could simply not imagine why Sidney Poitier was not good enough, simply because he was Black. I also could not understand why Irina and Stan were not good enough, just because they were Gypsies.

Since I never understood the workings of the world, I only realized certain things when I went to school. There was a Gypsy woman at the corner of our school who was selling sunflower seeds and making some money that way. I will never forget the day when the following scene happened. I was with a group of school friends on my way home when the Gypsy woman moved towards us asking if we wanted to buy some sunflower seeds from her. Not only did my friends stop walking, but everybody made a step backwards while I was the only one moving towards the woman. I asked her how expensive it was. It just so happened that I had the few leis she wanted. I bought, I ate, and I enjoyed. I was shocked about my friends and my friends were shocked about me.

Little did I know that the system expected me not only to think badly of the Gypsy woman, but I was supposed to refuse her in an aggressive way and make her feel like trash. But had I known what was expected of me, it still would not have happened. Let alone since I was not even aware of the expectations. When I arrived home, my Mom asked me why I was not hungry for lunch and I told her that I had had some delicious sunflower seeds from our school's Gypsy woman. My Mom told me to say when I was hungry again. I have to tell you that the Gypsy lady from that day on always gave me my portion of delicious sunflower seeds for free.

I do not know how I would have reacted had it not been for Mama Ana, Irina and Stan. Why do I mention the Gypsies in connection with religion and spirituality? I do not want to appear naive. I am aware that there is no official religion of the Gypsies. And at the time of my childhood they were talked about in connection to magic. I didn't understand what that meant. I never experienced any ritual and to this day I feel I know nothing about that aspect of being a Gypsy. It only made me sad to see that grown-ups did not like them based on criteria I did not agree with. I am very happy that under my life circumstances at that time I even managed to love the Gypsies!

5 JEWS: "NOT ENOUGH JEWISH BREAD AT THE SYNAGOGUE?"

As if my appreciation of Gypsies were not enough, I also have an admiration for the Jews. On the same floor with us I had a friend who was a few years older than me and who was a Jew. Her name was Natalia. I was only one-year-old when I met Natalia for the first time and, of course, I had no idea about her and her family's religion. I only remember how nice Natalia was and how devastatingly sad she was the day her dad died. She came running to talk to my mom who offered her the kindest words. I was very sad for Natalia and her family and I was sad for myself for not being invited to Natalia's dad's funeral. When I mildly protested by asking my mom why we were not invited to his funeral, she only answered matter of factly, "Because we do not have the right religion." I did not have any religion, right or wrong. And why was I being kept away from Natalia's dad's funeral while otherwise I always attended them?

This was the first time that I heard that people could have such a thing as the right or the wrong religion. I suppose I was about ten at that time. Natalia being as sweet as she was, once a year (please don't ask me when exactly, but I think it was in the spring) she used to bring us some Jewish bread from the synagogue on a special Jewish holiday whose name I do not know to this day. Year after year I enjoyed eating my Jewish bread, but I always found that my portion was way too small. I did not dare ask for more, although I felt like it. My mom had a philosophy that "You do not appear hungry even when you are" and "You do not ask for more just because you like it". So, in order to solve my dilemma, I came up with the following explanation: my portion of Jewish bread was so small, because the portion for my family was so small, because the portion for Natalia's family was so small, because there was never enough Jewish bread at the synagogue! Although I did not like the idea, at least it helped me accept my very small portion of Jewish bread.

Natalia will never know how much I would have enjoyed it if they had introduced larger portions at the synagogue. As I grew older, I realized that the Jews in Romania at the time of Ceausescu were left to their own devices and were even granted the right to go to Israel if they applied for immigration and followed the recommended standard procedure. I hope Natalia and her family is doing well in Israel.

Later in my life, I had the opportunity to meet different people of Jewish heritage at different times, and it always made me sad to think of such an important part of the world as Israel being out of peace and never understanding why. Maybe the day will come when harmony, joy, effortlessness, awareness, peace, balance, transcendence, insight, intelligence, prosperity, and success will touch the hearts of all good Jewish people and good Palestinians (and I know there are many of them both) and we will all rejoice in their joy of spiritual co-existence.

6 MOVING FROM ROMANIA TO AUSTRIA

My personal background is partially Romanian, partially Austrian and partially Italian. In the second half of the seventies my family and I left Romania to settle in Austria.

It was time to get to know more about my paternal grandfather's universe. I did not feel I knew much about Austria, only that they spoke German like the German minority in Romania and were Roman Catholics like the Hungarian minority in Romania. But the Austrians were neither Germans nor Hungarians. They were Germanic and Roman Catholic at the same time. Even at a young age I was comfortable with the German language, but that was only one aspect of my move from Romania to Austria. I didn't know enough about German-speaking countries, or their social, economic or religious culture.

My grandfather had never been very communicative about his Austrian heritage and at the same time I was never emotionally close to him. Even though we saw each other regularly, I remember him as a person who came across to me as a bit too aloof, too unapproachable and too uncomfortable to be around.

In Romania even though the political system was so inadequate, I grew up thinking that I discovered my tiny place in the universe. Even Communism could not hinder me from discovering my love of reading and my passion for writing. From day one I enjoyed going to school and was open to learning. (Much later in life an astrologer told me that there is a constellation in my horoscope that he interpreted as a sign that I was a soul who arrived for life-long learning. I was in my early thirties when he revealed this information to me and immediately it all made perfect sense. Yes, I did feel that I was a soul constantly open to learning.)

Going to school in Romania was a very positive experience for me as I could develop interests, talents and manifest my ambitions. I felt that as I would eventually grow up, I would continue to enjoy my tiny place within the universe. By the time I left Romania I had been selected into the circle of writers for my age group as a young teenager, and I enjoyed going to every meeting. In Romania I had also discovered my athletic talent for high jumping which was also reinforced by the system in special trainings and various athletic camps. At a certain point, I personally made a decision against athleticism in favor of pursuing a purely academic education. My parents accepted my decision without a problem, as even though I had passed my exam to enter and attend a special athletic school, when I told them I missed my old school and did not like the new one at all, I was allowed to return. Reading and writing meant a lot more to me than the high jump.

I took it for granted that even in the political context of my childhood I was able to discover myself on a deeper level. The system was inadequate in many ways, but whatever interest I displayed, there was always some resonance to it. I enjoyed my foreign languages, I enjoyed my magazines about the world of cinema, I enjoyed music and I enjoyed watching television. My childhood was full of American movies (among my favorite actors were Shirley MacLaine, Audrey Hepburn, Goldie Hawn, Grace Kelly, Jerry Lewis, and Danny Kaye, just to name a few), BBC productions of the great English classics (*David Copperfield, Jane Eyre, The Forsythe Saga, Emma, Elizabeth* R), Italian and French movies, music and entertainment shows (when Anna Magnani, my favorite Italian actress, died, I couldn't have cried more had she been a relative of mine, and my two favorite Italian singers were Gianni Morandi and Gigliola Cinquetti; Louis de Funés and Catherine Deneuve were my favorite French actors and Mireille Mathieu my favorite French singer).

After a long unintended and unexpected separation from the entertainment universe of my childhood, I was more than thrilled to reconnect by watching *BBC Prime, Rai Uno* and *TV5Monde.* As a grown-up all the positive emotions of my childhood came back to life and I understood why I had been fascinated by all these cultures even as a little girl. Each one of them brought me joy and a depth of life in its own unique and irreplaceable way.

In Romania, school reinforced all my academic interests and I have a fond memory of the vast majority of my Romanian teachers, who in my eyes had been both great teachers and great human beings. I need to add that I have always been field-independent, even though I only became aware of it when I studied psychology. As a field-independent student I loved the subject simply because I loved the subject independent of my teachers. Usually students, especially younger ones, make their likes and dislikes in school dependent on how much they like their teacher. I was never a victim of such dependence. Field-independence can also lead to unconventional behavior or even to a leadership personality instead of a follower personality. Put in simple terms, the field-independent person does not care much about other people's opinions and stays focused on their primary object of interest.

In Romania not only was I was allowed to practice my field-independence, but I feel that I was reinforced in this. I suppose that freedom was possible because my personal ambitions were all academic and I was a very mild child. What somebody else might have experienced if they had been radical and/or aggressive, I cannot say. I was never wild and I felt very comfortable with myself and my surroundings, be they within the family or within the system.

Practically from one day to the next, I lost the emotional comfort, the academic familiarity and the effortless meaningfulness of my life in Romania, to move to Austria. I regained the feeling that indeed there is a right place for me within the universe, only after I entered the American system a few years later. Once again motivation, ambition and achievement were all encouraged and rewarded. As my life felt finally meaningful again, I was also equipped with a higher purpose, especially now that freedom on so many levels was truly a part of my experience.

7 THE ROMAN CATHOLIC CHURCH AND JUNGSCHAR

Jung in German means young and Schar means a group of people usually connected to religious activities. For example, Jesus always had a big Schar of people around him while he was preaching. Jungschar refers to the groups of young people in the Roman Catholic Church.

I had my first encounter with the Jungschar shortly after my move to Austria when my friends from school asked me one day if I was interested in joining them. Of course, I was. I had no idea what it was all about, but as I've always been open to new experiences, I wouldn't have missed going to Jungschar to experience it on my own. The meetings took place in a building next to one of the Roman Catholic churches and in my opinion they were basically social gatherings where grown-ups helped the younger ones with some charity projects or some social events, often before major religious holidays. I found everybody very nice, the activities meaningful and enjoyed going to Jungschar when my school work allowed.

While all my friends lived close to the school and to their church, I wonder why I was put into a school so far away from my home. I lived too far away to be able to join the Jungschar regularly. I have the most pleasant memories from my visits to the Jungschar, but since life is not meant to be pleasant for a Roman Catholic and their friends like me, more was to happen to complete my view regarding this oldest institution of Christianity.

Not only did my parents put me into a school that was far away from home, but on top of that it was also an all-girls school. Was I already half a Roman Catholic? And what did the two of them have in mind for me long-term? A monastery?

Just before Christmas, the whole class went to church for mass. I was entering a Roman Catholic church for the very first time at that point and my positive Jungschar experiences did not prepare me well for participating in a Roman Catholic mass. Not knowing what to do, I sat down on one of the mightily uncomfortable benches. After waiting for a number of minutes, I saw that I was the only one sitting while all the other girls stood in a long line.

As if that was not strange enough already, some of them looked absolutely frightened, some of them held their hands as if they were praying for mercy and others were simply unnaturally mute. My best friend Sylvia, who had invited me to the Jungschar, saw that I did not know the procedural workings. She came to me and asked me, "Don't you have anything to confess?"

"Confess? What?"

Sylvia was apparently very disappointed by my complete ignorance and said in the most indignant tone, "Your sins!"

There were so many contradictory questions running to my head that I am sure to Sylvia I must have looked as if I came from another world. The truth is I did on all possible levels. I first looked at that long queue and it started to dawn on me what they were doing there. We were all girls of about 14-15 years, seriously getting ready for confessions. I asked myself: "Who am I spending my days with in school if every single girl has so much to confess?" Sylvia was still waiting for me to stand up from the bench and join the crowd. I had never been in such a situation before in my life, but I felt it was best to follow and obey. I went to the end of the queue. At least Sylvia was happy with me.

As I wondered about the sins of the others, I realized that I was in major trouble. I had no sins to confess. I had not lied, I had not stolen, I had not killed, I had not had sex, I had not had anything to offer that could have been regarded as a sin. The only thing that changed between then and now is about having sex and that I never regarded as a sin. At about 15 I was truly unaware what I could present to the priest as sinful. I realized I truly did not know the rules of this game.

There are many absurd things in our world and having me at 15 make up a story in this context is one of them. I felt I would have needed some lessons in illegal and/or immoral behaviors before having to show up. Probably watching *Godfather II* would have helped, but I was unaware of that movie at that time. I do not even know if it had already been produced. So I quickly improvised. When my turn came I told the priest the truth. My mother found me ungrateful, rude and impatient. I had no idea if I was all these things, but I think quoting one's own mom is the most adequate source of sins. I did not know where else to turn. I wondered if there were also references needed from my father's side who never had any complaints against me. I know in his eyes I was never ungrateful, rude or impatient. But thank god the priest did not ask and so I did not have to offer anything. Even if my mother was right, being ungrateful, rude and impatient does not exactly equate to breaking one of the ten commandments. I was fully aware of that even then, but what was I supposed to do to successfully comply with the demands?

Communism was very perverse in many of its demands, but I found that the demands of the Roman Catholic Church topped even that. The entire inner process I went through had a very negative effect on me and it forced me to develop a sense of skepticism regarding Roman Catholic beliefs and attitudes. I stopped going to Jungschar and I never again joined my class for mass. I suppose the depression rate of Roman Catholic priests is an uninvestigated topic, so as not to say a well-hidden secret. People who have to listen to stories like mine on a regular basis can only become seriously depressed by the triviality and absurdity of the exchange in the course of time, and I wanted no share in such a phenomenon. As I grew older I wondered what a Roman Catholic upbringing did to the self-worth and self-image of someone? I only knew I wanted that type of upbringing to stay out of my life. I was myself a grown-up when other adults opened up about their Roman Catholic childhood and all the traumas it left behind. I was shocked on the one hand by their many sad experiences, and on the other hand by my blatant ignorance about this phenomenon, which I had never encountered before either as a child or as an adult.

Turning into a young adult surrounded by the Roman Catholic morphogenetic field in Austria was stranger than my childhood during Communism. At least in Romania the official layer of how to handle the system was paralleled by the unofficial layer of inner freedom to keep the system at a distance. In Austria people only had an official layer, without the choice of being able to create an emotional and spiritual buffer zone. Again and again I saw people my age, and also older generations, tormented by considerations fueled by religious misunderstandings and contradictions. They often put themselves in situations that I would call "lose-lose" instead of the ideal "win-win".

As I traveled around Europe, I realized that the Italians and French, who are also Catholics, place a lot of emphasis on enjoying life to the maximum. Seemingly so do the Spanish that I never visited, but got to know in person at different points in time. Could it be that combining Germanic and Catholic influences has the most disadvantageous interaction effect? How come that the Mediterranean countries give themselves the freedom of having a lifestyle full of pleasure, be it in their cuisine, be it in their fashion, or be it in their passion for life in general? What breaks a Germanic Roman Catholic to the point where life for them is seemingly only about guilt, martyrdom, missionarism, arrogance and passive aggression?

My brush with Roman Catholicism during my teenage years came to an abrupt end, but I feel it was the only option for me. When I went to Rome in 1986, I wanted to visit the Vatican - not for religious, but for cultural reasons. As we were waiting to enter, we were rejected because my summer dress was backless. I knew the pope would not be there in person and we were considered good enough to pay entrance, but other than that the masses are always only filling material. I had already learned this from Communism. I wondered what the Roman Catholic Church was all about if mere bare shoulders were too much to cope with for its clergy?

That day in Rome, it all came back to me. All the atrocities over the centuries committed by this institution out of date and out of touch with real life of real people. History came to life in front of my eyes as I was rejected, and I comprehended for the very first time the power of misunderstanding and abuse. In 2005 when the pope died I was forced by circumstances to watch the ceremony of his funeral on television, and while the neighbors in my room reacted as if this event was the biggest loss in human history, I only thought to myself in my hospital bed, "You apparently most modest man, in your most modest coffin, I still cannot stop thinking of you as the world's first and greatest businessman ever!" And when at the end of 2007 the new pope proclaimed something like the significance of the revival of exorcism, I also caught myself thinking something nasty: "You must know exactly what you are talking about because your clergy bunch seems to be in the greatest need of winning the battle against their own inner demons, and stopping their favorite hobby of polishing each other's halos!"

8 THE NEO-PROTESTANTS

Neo-Protestants were for me like an unexpected oasis in the middle of the Roman Catholic desert. When I received the Americans' invitation to go to their church with them, I was as always open to do so. I knew very little about Neo-Protestants at that time.

In Romania during Communism it was not a good idea to be a Neo-Protestant. As soon as people gave a higher meaning to their relationship with divinity, the system reacted with a strong allergy to it. I had known neighbors who as Neo-Protestants faced discrimination in their workplace and were told not to activate their colleagues to become members of their church. They could not be stopped from attending, but once they started recruiting, things became unpleasant for them. Any public discourse ended up in prison and with a loss of all social contacts. It was almost impossible to be a happy Neo-Protestant while lacking freedom.

Living now in freedom I was even more curious about Neo-Protestants and their ways. Compared to the mechanical rituals of the Romanian Orthodox church which bordered sometimes on the superstitious and the scary expectations and dogma of the Roman Catholic church which bordered on the unnatural, listening to a Neo-Protestant pastor made unexpected sense! The quotations from the Bible were connected and came to life in pragmatic ways that I had never been aware of before. I was happy to realize that between latent emptiness and manifest horror there was something significantly valuable about the teachings of Jesus and his philosophy. The way my American friends led their lives, the way they interacted with one another both at church and outside, the way they brought up their children, the way they regarded life in general, the way they valued the conscious connection to divinity, all these factors became a very powerful source of practical inspiration to me.

Going to Bible study groups made me happy. I am not sure how I felt while going to church in Romania. Let's say I was definitely not unhappy, maybe more neutral than anything else. The church had no effect on me because I never attended mass, I was only present for the ceremonies of baptism, marriage and funeral. I do know how I felt going to a Roman Catholic church, and I was most unhappy. While the Romanian Orthodox church had a highly impersonal touch to it, attending the Roman Catholic church became highly personal by the silly obligation of confession. Having to tell a complete stranger about private circumstances unrelated to anything important felt perverse, and all the ideas about authority and absolution were entirely lost on me. However, it was a special treasure for me to be in an American church and simply happy. All of a sudden divinity was presented to me in a positive perspective where the focus was not all on fear, denial or punishment. What a difference all that makes!

I would like to mention that for me being happy and being unhappy are two very important states. If you found the redundancy annoying, it is only because I cannot think of a better dichotomy to describe how church made me feel. It was not about sadness or anger or oppression, and also not about fear or damnation but simply about happiness.

I am not saying that Neo-Protestants are completely free of fear, denial or punishment, but compared to all other Christian denominations they have the smallest portions of them. I experienced far fewer contradictions and tensions when it came to their everyday life concepts and attitudes. There was something very peaceful about Neo-Protestant philosophy and the powerful guidance it offered for all life contexts. For the very first time I discovered that modern authors wrote books explaining biblical principles and applying them to current issues of human concern. While Martin Luther (1483-1546) freed the old German states from the slavery of the pope (around 1517-1520) and Henry VIII (1491-1547) did the same for England by breaking with Rome (around 1533-1540), it was the Neo-Protestants who brought Christianity to the next higher level (although the Anglicans did very well for themselves in the course of history, and if I had to name one event that facilitated the exponential rise to power of the Jewel-Island, then I trace it back to the liberation from Roman Catholicism).

For the first time in my life the Americans showed me that you can aspire to a conscious connection to divinity and have a great life without being burdened by self-sabotage and self-punishment. Maybe at that time I would not have been able to use the same words that I put in writing now, but being a Neo-Protestant is about alignment to divinity's most positive qualities in a grounded way. Neo-Protestants allow divinity to accompany them every step of the way, at all times and under all circumstances, in the most practical way. There is a lot more congruence between theory and practice in Neo-Protestant beliefs than all others. This is not to say that improvements are not needed or welcomed. Even if Neo-Protestants have the smallest portions of prejudice and judgment, I am aware that they are not completely free of them.

If I needed to name two concepts which I experienced in a very different light with Neo-Protestants, then I would mention trust and success. While other Christians have an ambivalent relationship to trust, bordering on distrust, Neo-Protestants more easily create a relational bond in which trust occupies a bigger space. Regarding success the Neo-Protestants are the ones who seem to openly practice their aspiration to success, their recognition of success and their gratification of success. There is no feeling of guilt in wanting to be successful or enjoying it once it comes. The other Christians prefer the mask of false modesty and pretend to put down attempts at success and especially triumphs.

Energetically, trust is generated and sustained by the female aspect, while success is generated and sustained by the male aspect. In humans these two factors are determined by our relationships to our mother and our father. I need to wonder if Neo-Protestants perpetuate parental relationships that are significantly different in their quantity and their quality from the types of relationships found amongst people who are not Neo-Protestant? I am not sure about the right answer to all these questions, I just intuitively feel there might be a significant difference.

Aside from trust and success, which can be regarded as the foundation, I would also like to mention the concept of self-empowerment that makes such a difference in how far we allow ourselves as grown-ups to be fully mature and self-determined. Neo-Protestants experience the unlimited existence of resources and this enables them to fulfill their potential on a higher scale than someone who functions within given boundaries and frames and never steps outside the box. The practical application of all these concepts makes a difference not only on the individual, but also on the societal level. Neo-Protestants as a society focus on contributing and giving and this attitude is the seed of progress and improvement in all areas of human lives.

9 THE QUAKERS

If I regarded the Neo-Protestants as a macrocosm, then I regarded the Quakers as a microcosm. I never knew any Neo-Protestant family as closely as I got to know my Quakers. Therein lies for me the difference between macro and micro.

If it is true that knowledge has three different levels – the first being "I know what I know!", the second being "I know what I do not know!", and the third being "I do not know what I do not know!" – then Communism is about not knowing what one does not know, and on top of that about being kept exactly at that level. When my Austrian friends disclosed to me that they were Quakers, I needed to admit to them that I had not even heard the word before, but I was thankful to leave the third level of knowledge for the second one.

I am not sure if this particular family of friends were so special specifically because they were Quakers or if they would have been just as special independent of any religious affiliation, but since religion seems to make such a difference in human life I suppose that I was dealing with a significant interaction effect. This was in the fact that they were special and that being Quaker reinforced all their special qualities.

Compared to all other religious people, this family mentioned being Quaker just from time to time. It was not something I heard from them on an everyday basis. I remember that the first context in which being a Quaker became significant was when it came to going to the military or doing civil service instead. I learned then that Quakers are pacifists and do not go to war. It was clear that the young man in the family who would need to make a choice between military and civil service, would decide on civil service based on religious belief. Peace was one of the major priorities of Quakers. I could understand then why they were all so harmonious within their family and within the outside world. I had known them for at least one year at that point and I spent my weekends and most of my vacations visiting them. They were not just paying lip service to some abstract concept, but they were a living proof of it. I was very impressed.

Another year later the next context in which being a Quaker became relevant was in connection to their attitude to social responsibility. The mother in the family got involved in a project to help underprivileged children with learning disabilities. She regarded her involvement as her civic duty and she would not close her eyes to the need of others if she was in a position to help. Regarding Quakers there are things in the category of "what they are all about" and there are things in the category of "what they are not about". The list might read like labels of supplements which contain certain ingredients, but at the same time do not contain others. The Quaker beliefs did not contain superstition, missionarism, co-dependency, denial, narcissism, or hidden agendas. I was puzzled by the combination of things the Quakers were not about. I was in my late teens at that time and I regard my close contacts to this family of Quakers as a profoundly formative period for my life. To an outsider they might have sounded a bit utopian, but to me they were very grounded and very real.

At the beginning of my friendship with them, I repeatedly came back home and shared with my family some of my new insights about life. Unfortunately, neither my mom nor my dad understood me, but rather rejected my experiences as "theoretical". Although I would have really enjoyed sharing my new knowledge with them, which meant so much to me, at some point I felt I needed to give up. As I internalized new values, I was criticized more and more within my own family. I was regarded as either idealistic or unrealistic, or viewed as the black sheep in the family for my so-called snobbism. The whole situation reminded me vaguely of Mama Ana's destiny in our larger family. She had been unconventional, but highly successful in everything she did. Above all things she committed the unforgivable crime of becoming the richest member of the family. She was exposed to envy and heavy criticism, and sometimes as I realized much later as a grown-up, even to hate. Mama Ana had been the only person in my childhood who had instilled in me the concept of excellence and quality. All her life she was a no-nonsense-woman with very high expectations of herself and all others around her. She had been a very kind soul, highly intelligent and generous, but at the same time not willing to take responsibility for other people's shortcomings which caused an enormous resistance in her closer circle. While knowing my family of Quakers, in most aspects I rarely caught myself thinking they were "Just like Mama Ana!", however when I thought of standards of excellence and quality, I did. Mama Ana was never particularly influenced by religious conventions. She was an original soul full of spirituality. On the other hand, the Quakers held onto their religion and it was their guiding light. Although separated by religion, they were united by their common belief in quality and excellence. As I got to know the family better, I realized that my resonance with them had its roots in the positive influence of my grandmother.

The Quakers further enriched my life in two additional areas: problem-solving and decision-making. Regarding problem-solving, they had a deep inner knowledge that represented a combination between the energetic and the cognitive. They did not practice any philosophy based on energy, but to me they were unconsciously energetically aware of things. They were very creative and highly differentiated in their approaches to all issues that needed a solution. Regarding decision-making, they had a highly intelligent system of defining priorities. Everything they did was a function of choice, not necessity. They moved through life on an everyday basis with the least resistance I had ever seen. They were full of harmony and joy and kept a positive focus regarding all aspects of everyday life. It was more than mind-opening for me to see them organize things and experience them. They were very hard-working and at the same time they enjoyed life to the maximum. Social gatherings with friends and cultural events were integrated on a regular basis, but without any touch of pushiness or compulsion. There was never anything obsessive about the Quakers. At all times they were fully alive and constantly in the flow of energies. Externally, they did things just like everybody else, but internally they had special attitudes that set them apart from the rest. Had I been able to only observe them from the outside without having any information about them, I would have thought they were Buddhists. Maybe there is an overlap between Quakers and Buddhists, but I have never heard the comparison being made. Perhaps I am only projecting my own bits and pieces of knowledge that cannot serve as a foundation for a valid conclusion. Of course, they were not fully like Buddhists for the fact that they were integrated within society just like everybody else. Typically, when we think of Buddhists in the Western world, we think about the monks in their long orange robes who possess nothing and spend their lives meditating in a monastery. My Quakers did not have anything to do with that Buddhist aspect of life.

It was impressive to see them function in the outside world being carried by a philosophy that made such a positive difference to all of them and all the people they touched. They incorporated a high level of congruence between thinking, feeling and acting. They had both a spiritual identity and a spiritual character. There was something powerfully healing about my contact with them. The interactions of family members with each other were always respectful and based on trust. Everything they did was to reinforce that trust and avoid any breach of trust. I had never been treated better in my entire life by a whole family. Everything was full of fairness, freedom, and kindness. The family placed a special emphasis on education, as all adults were highly educated and always open to learning in all its various forms. And there was one more aspect that was significantly different from everything else I had seen before. While most human interactions are about dominance and invalidation, especially by means of intimidation and humiliation, the interactions of the Quakers were always in the service of validating one's own experiences. I never felt put down even when critical questions were asked and my deeper processes were put to the test.

As the years passed I could not stop being in awe of the Quaker philosophy, and I wished more and more that my entire life had been defined by their philosophy from the very beginning. I was only left with the choice of letting the Quaker philosophy work for me in the future, which has never stopped. Their philosophy enriches every moment of life in the most harmonious and joyful way and reinforces my potential as a spiritual being on a constant basis. Problem-solving and decision-making in the Quakers' style has again and again made very significant differences in my personal life, and when people in my closer surroundings have been challenged by my problem-solving and my decision-making, I have simply recommended that they think that: "Oh, she's just having one of her mystical experiences again!" Too bad that for most people deeper levels of higher order problem-solving and decision-making remain a mystery!

10 PARAPSYCHOLOGY

When I was asked to teach a course in Parapsychology at an American university in Europe, I gladly accepted without knowing how enriching I would find the experience not only for my students but for myself as well. (Parapsychology is defined as the discipline that investigates the existence and causes of psychic abilities and phenomena, even though such events cannot be accounted for by natural law and are based on information that could have been obtained through the usual sensory abilities.) As the weekend for teaching my class approached, however, I started feeling an enormous resistance which I had not known before and which became so bad that my body developed a fever and we had to cancel. I told the organizer to reschedule by giving me at least two or three weekends before having to teach again. Something was going on with me that placed me in a situation that caused me to have a dilemma.

I knew I loved the topic of parapsychology. I knew it was a topic close to my heart and soul. I was also aware I had spoken about parapsychology in an informal way before, but I had no idea why I was reacting with such an unusual resistance when it came to teaching a formal class. It was interesting to observe how my physical body took responsibility for my process, by drawing attention to the fact that I was out of balance. When I told the organizer to give me time with the rescheduling, I was not worried about my physical body because I knew the fever would be gone within the shortest time, but I felt highly motivated to understand the deeper level of my own process. There was something very important going on and I could feel it even though I could not put it into words. On the one hand I was the intellectual asked to teach - an activity I have always loved doing. (As a matter of fact friends of mine who are familiar with astrology told me that in my horoscope they can see the constellation for my teaching talent, a fact which was confirmed in my life by being invited by two different people independent of one another to open up schools, which sadly never happened due to practical reasons.) On the other hand, I was the intuitive being born with a capacity to feel energies and aware of many phenomena - phenomena that most people do not have access to but that are to a huge extent a part of my everyday life ever since I can remember. As I could not teach that original weekend I started to realize what my problem really was. My preparation had been, to put it mildly, very superficial. It was as if I had decided that my students could only get a homeopathic dosage of parapsychology. I wondered why I had made that decision in the first place, and why I had not been aware of it.

What was the missing link in understanding my resistance? I was motivated, I was knowledgeable, but... what else? I was also extremely torn. The ancient Taoists say that we have the thinking brain in our head and the feeling brain in our solar plexus. This is the only concept that comes to mind which helps me explain my state at that point. My thinking brain and my feeling brain were at war!! But why?

I was myself a walking parapsychological phenomenon, so what was my internal fuss about? It took me days to understand myself, but before my insight came, I really felt completely lost. I hate the state of feeling lost and since the saying goes that each problem carries within it the solution, I helped myself by using parapsychology. I realized I was dealing with a very deep trauma on my side and I could only solve my crisis by going into some of my past lives. Reincarnation therapy was the key for me as I realized that women who had been intuitive and in touch with nature and maybe even in a social position of significant power often also got in trouble for it and made the decision never to speak up again. There I was, a victim of my own parapsychological talents and interests from so many ages ago! I was one of the women who had made a decision not to speak up again and how could I have imagined being able to teach when I was still traumatized and in serious need of healing? What was I expecting would happen to me? Would I be stoned to death or burned as a witch or buried alive? The whole process was incredible: first, how an unresolved trauma from the past can haunt us for so many centuries; second, how it affects our present in such a negative way; third, what it takes to transcend the crisis of the past and bring freedom into the present; fourth, how the tools are available to us when we have the consciousness for them; fifth, how our individual level gets transformed at the root of the problem instead of on a purely cosmetic level (which would have only addressed my physical body's fever); and sixth, how planetary consciousness can be achieved by humankind! Oh, oops, I forget... Number six is still work in progress, but who knows? Maybe one day...?

I cannot put into words how much energy came to me after I resolved the issue of my resistance. Of course, I immediately made the conscious decision to speak up and speak out. I threw away the superficial preparation, that of a traumatized and unhealed human and created the syllabus of the self-empowered and self-determined soul. I felt ready to speak and so I did. Although the syllabus also included writings about telepathy for espionage purposes, clairvoyant participation for crime investigations and religiously inspired bleedings recognized by the Roman Catholic Church, the most memorable materials came first, from ancient Egypt and all its cultural treasures, especially the power of their pyramids; second, from Paramahansa Yolgananda's *Autobiography of a Yogi*, one of the books that I was extremely sorry to get to the last page of; third, from, the book *If You Meet the Buddha on the Road, Kill Him!* whose author I cannot remember, but that had an enlightening effect on me; fourth, from, *Hands of Light* by Barbara Ann Brennan whom I had experienced in person at a seminar in the States and whom I would not have omitted from my syllabus for the world; and fifth, from the two books whose authors I don't remember *The Celestine Prophecy* and *The Way of the Shaman*.

I know the last sentence was extremely long, and I pondered a lot if I should not reformulate it. According the energies, the information contained in it represents an entire universe. Why fragment it when fragmentation is one of the illnesses of our world? Upon enough consideration I decided to flow with the energies instead of applying rules which can be meaningful but have to be expanded into exceptions when the situation requires it. It is ironic and it makes me laugh that I wrote the longest sentence of my entire writing career in my very first public piece! I did not plan to do it, it just happened. Let the critics pay attention to such details, I will stay focused on my message, my style and my voice when putting my thoughts on paper for everybody to read. That is the way I am and I need to stay the way I am. It is good to know all the rules and it is even better to know when to ignore them.

Regarding teaching Parapsychology - that I opened up was quite miraculous, but at the same time that my students also opened up was just as miraculous. We all had our own version of *In Search of the Miraculous*, even though we all agreed that none of us understood a word of what Ouspenky and Gurdjieff were really talking about. I wish I could have kept all my students' papers which were excellent and highly parapsychological, describing personal experiences, phenomena and insights. Who would have thought that in the mid-nineties the world was latently parapsychological?

11 MOTHER MEERA

I heard about Mother Meera for the very first time while in the States and a friend of mine shared with me a book written by one of Mother Meera's students. In his book he described a very intense energetic process which reminded me of previous readings. After finishing the book, my friend told me that Mother Meera lived in Europe at the time and I made a plan to visit her once I was back.

The day I arrived for my very first darshan, I was so excited and felt very fortunate. At the hotel, all the others had been at Mother Meera's before and were thrilled to be back. People came from all over the world. Energetically, I could feel the incredible frequency and I knew I was in the right place at the right time. It was not the same level of knowing, the way we know logical things, but it was a form of inner knowing on a very deep level. Embedded in this very special frequency, I left with the group to experience the darshan premiere. All I knew at that point was that everybody would sit completely quietly while Mother Meera would work with every guest individually for a few minutes by placing her hands on the head or other parts of the body. Our group was very large and it felt like it was going to be a big event.

Once I stepped into Mother Meera's house, it felt like home in the energetic sense. I had had a few of these experiences in my life before, but this one felt very powerful. Within a few seconds, so much information came to me that I was amazed that communication with the spiritual world could be so fast. Usually the connection is slower, at least for me, and the chunks of information are in smaller portions.

I noticed a lady and I immediately felt that I should have run to her to give her a big hug and say, "Here I am again! Finally back!" Needless to say, I wondered about my own mental sanity. I really needed to keep myself under control to not do it. I stood there glued to the floor trying to integrate what was happening. After the lady disappeared for half a minute she came back, stopped a few meters in front of me, looked me in the eye and said to me, "You are here for the first time." I was so stunned that I could not say anything on the physical level, but I know I asked her telepathically, "Do you also know me? Do you recognize me?" On the physical level she only smiled and I felt like she was giving me the hug I wanted to share with her, and was welcoming me back.

Again for half a minute she disappeared, came back to me and said: "Please wait here until I come to get you!" I would not have done otherwise for the world. I was still in awe. I only knew another level of consciousness took over. People were moving around trying to find a place for the darshan. From what they said I understood that my lady was Mother Meera's assistant. I had never felt more at peace or more at home in the energetic sense in many lifetimes. After everybody else seemed to have found their places, my lady came back to me and gesticulated to me to follow her. She took me into the big room and said to me: "This is your place!" and made me sit down. I said thank you and happily sat down. Within a few minutes, somebody tried to sit in front of me, but my lady came and told this person: "You cannot sit here! Come with me!" When Mother Meera came and sat down, I realized that I had been given the very best place by my lady! I could still not integrate the many unusual events that took place in such a short time. I only felt the incredible flow of energy and the power of my experience.

Now, Mother Meera started giving her blessing at the other end of the room and I knew I was going to be among the last ones to get my turn. I felt I needed that time to let the energy sink in before I was touched by Mother Meera. All the participants were very quiet, very disciplined and very happy. I was beyond time and space. I cannot identify more because I do not know the words. After a certain number of hours, my turn came to move in front of Mother Meera, and as if I had not already experienced more than enough mysticism for a million lifetimes, even more was to come my way. When I looked into Mother Meera's eyes, I burst out in laughter which I just could not control. Mother Meera was not surprised, she gave a faint smile and continued looking at me while the others were shocked. I did not know what I was anymore or if I was at all anymore. I only felt that while I was looking into Mother Meera's eyes, I met divinity. And not only that I met divinity, but that that state was very familiar to me. My linear mind tried to suggest to me the unforgivable faux pas I had committed by bursting out in laughter. I heard Mother Meera say on the energetic level "Nonsense!" and the suggestion against me vanished into the ether. I could have stayed like that for ages, but the physical plain is not for eternity. When the time felt right to her, Mother Meera sent me back to my place.

I suppose when words fail us that is when we humans reach that spiritual dimension we were meant to embody from the very beginning. It was the very first time at that darshan that I experienced the meaning of just being. I know it had nothing to do with me as a human being, but was facilitated to me by Mother Meera's consciousness. She gave me an incredible, unexpected and unique present by sharing with me for a moment the immensity of divinity by using her consciousness as the bridge between the worlds.

After integrating my experience many weeks later, I felt compelled to ask myself why India is in the state it is in? What happened to this ancient culture that I regard as the sleeping princess of the world that put herself to sleep for all the wrong reasons? How can India on the one hand be the origin of pure divine consciousness for some people, while on the other hand for so many others remain the place of poverty, passivity and helplessness? Princess India, Sleeping Beauty of the world, wake up! Wake up to your wisdom, to your potential, to your mission! You are the Princess of the world who can liberate herself from all the social conventions that keep you enslaved to old patterns!

I wish everybody could have experienced what I experienced at my first darshan. Not only would we all feel that the world is saved, but we would also all realize that our world was never meant to be in another state.

12 "SAMURAI!"

Having suffered through the difficulties of learning the Hiragana alphabet by no means makes me an expert of Japanese culture, but since I was so fascinated by everything that came from so far away, I could not resist attempting to learn Japanese. From my childhood in Romania I remember watching Japanese movies on television and having a very strange reaction regarding the effect Japanese men and Japanese women had on me. When the ladies spoke I felt very comfortable, but when the men spoke I usually became scared (I need to add in Romania to this day the movies are always presented in their original language). Why gender had such a powerful effect on me when it came to Japanese movies, I do not know.

In my early twenties I was happy to be able to find time to start learning Japanese with a Japanese teacher. She was one of the gentlest people I have ever met. By profession she was a piano player from Japan living in Europe. I cannot exactly explain logically why I felt so attracted to Japanese culture, I just knew there was something for me to discover. About fifteen years later I found the answer. At that time, I was at a crossroads in need of redefinition and reorientation. I felt challenged by some of the situations life presented to me and felt that logic alone could not offer me the solution. In my usual habit, I went into a meditation and even at the beginning of my relaxation I felt there was a very powerful message coming my way. My soul guided me through the experience which on the one hand made me aware of my human dimension with all its confusion and limitation, and on the other hand of my spiritual dimension full of wisdom and infinity. Turning inwards had been my habit for a very long time and I cannot express enough my gratitude to the universe for allowing me to have this access. I remember looking for guidance regarding something new, that would make the feeling that I was in a constant inescapable free fall stop. I needed a new insight that would help me cope more easily with all the external changes which at times seemed unpredictable and overwhelming.

My soul took me to a beautiful landscape which already indicated the richness of the resources within me and made me slowly walk to a river. I followed the instruction without doubt or reservation and was curious what was expected of me by the time I reached the river. I moved closer and saw in front of my eyes how a bridge started to connect the two banks of the river. I felt very relieved because I knew the bridge was the symbol of what had been missing, the bridge between a familiar past that was obsolete and an unfamiliar future that could not wait to get started and did not seem to ask me if I was ready. I thought I needed to cross the bridge, but in my hurry my soul unexpectedly stepped in and said, "You have to stop here now!" I was surprised. What now? There was a split second of uncertainty on my human side, but even if I ever doubted myself, I never doubted my soul! So I stopped and listened. In front of my eyes, the bridge became more and more sophisticated, but it is difficult to put into words what I mean. I only remember it was made of wood, an element which is alive, and it grew into more detailed decoration and symbolism. I was already in awe of all the changes of my bridge beyond my thinking and volition. I felt I had received the guidance I was looking for, but while I was coming to an end on some level, two things happened simultaneously in this meditation; in the middle of the bridge a figure materialized out of thin air and my soul said in the clearest and loudest voice: "Samurai!" I could not have been more surprised!

To this day, which is approximately ten years later, I can hear my soul's clear and loud voice pronouncing "Samurai!" in a tone that implies the right attitude, the right value and the right action, all condensed in a single archetype. I have had many powerful experiences in my meditations, but this one was among the few ones which carried with it one of the most powerful, transformational and profound effects I have ever known. The frequency of the archetype of the Japanese Samurai is one of the highest I have ever encountered on the energetic level. Probably on the human level only a certain number of Samurais embodied that frequency, but the Japanese Samurai as an ideal is an aspect of each soul.

If there ever was a gift of the magi to all humankind, then it is the symbolism of the Samurai. Usually, the more powerful the message of a meditation, the longer I need to integrate it. It took me a long time by my standard to integrate the effect of that meditation. As things started to fall into the right place internally, I experienced significant changes externally in my interactions with challenging situations and unpredictable events. "Samurai!" transforms for me every challenge into a joyful learning experience.

On the human level I cannot claim to know much

about a Samurai, but on the energetic level I aspire to that frequency every day of my life. If I will ever manage to speak Japanese well (with Hiragana, Katagana and Kanji among my best friends) which of course I would love to do, or even if not, the real luxury of life for me lies in the gift of the "Samurai!" I regard it as the gift of the magi not only to me, but to all of us who care about spirituality.

13 THE ROMANIAN ORTHODOX CHURCH AFTER THE FALL OF THE IRON CURTAIN

It was about twenty years after my move that I felt yet another call back to my human roots of my present incarnation again. Two special experiences come to mind as I reflect upon Romanian spirituality. Friends of mine in the Romanian mountains invited me to go to their local church one Sunday morning. They had also arranged for me to speak to the Romanian pastor.

Right when I woke up that Sunday, I knew I was going to have a transformational experience in church. The energy felt like the death of a certain aspect of life and the birth of a new aspect. It coincided magnificently with the personal process I was going through.

As we came closer to the church, I could only see the top and I immediately noticed an aura full of light and peace. As the entire building became visible, the aura of light and peace intensified exponentially. I had known it was going to be a special experience and there it was. I felt tears coming down my cheeks, but knew it would have made no sense to try to control them. The aura of the church pulled me to it like a magical magnet. As I entered the church people looked at me as if I came from another world. They were polite and greeted me, but I was already half in a hypnotic state and could not respond to them. I could hardly see them as the light surrounded me and a feeling of peace made me cry even more. I must have looked strange, but there was nothing I could do about it.

Within the shortest time, the pastor came to greet us and I explained to him how moved I was by the energy of his church. He was impressed that I noticed. It would have been impossible for someone like me not to notice. We had a profound interaction regarding practical aspects of my life and the philosophical considerations of our connection to divinity.

During my conversation with him I broke down in tears and he later told my friends he had never seen anyone cry like me his entire life! My experience was completely cathartic. I understood why the church had such special energies when I met the pastor and interacted with him. He was truly a living link between the heavens and earth. His frequency was so high that his mere presence caused all the blockages to dissolve. I cannot exactly say what had burdened me to such a tremendous degree, but whatever it was, that heavy and intense energy left me by the time I stepped out of that church.

My body showed a strange reaction of inner coldness, dizziness and tiredness within the first hours of our visit, but after a good night's sleep, I felt and I was reborn. I can hardly put into words my mystical experience, but I can say that I felt very blessed to be taken to this special place, to this special person at the right time. When we expect it least, life seems to have even more generous presents for us. It was that same summer that I found myself, upon the recommendation of friends, visiting a monastery where the resident monk Father Teo was renowned for his harmonizing energies. I could connect to him immediately and in his presence I could feel his profound and strong connection to divinity. I truly felt happy to meet such a special soul and spend a little bit of time in his presence. His energy stayed with me for a very long time and I enjoyed the high frequency every second of it.

Early that fall, a Romanian friend of mine asked me, "Have you heard? A Father Teo is coming to Vienna next week. Have you heard of him?" She was planning to go to church to meet him. I asked her what monastery Father Teo came from and she could identify him as my Father Teo. The following day I called the church to tell the regular pastor that I had heard about Father Teo's visit and I asked to be put on the list for a home visit during his stay in Vienna.

They both came, our regular pastor and Father Teo and we had the most amazing encounter, laughter and fun on the highest spiritual level. I could not express my gratitude enough that once again the universe provided me with such a rich experience of blessing and happiness. At the end of his visit, I told Father Teo in my immodest way that he came to Vienna only for me. He laughed and didn't want to accept it, but I countered. "I know I am right!"

Sometime later our regular pastor asked me why I didn't show up in church more often. I told him that I found the service to be much too long, much too redundant and without a learning effect at the end of it. I told him that I preferred, when sitting in church, to know more about god at the end of the service than at the beginning. I told him I was expecting a learning effect, the kind I had experienced with the Neo-Protestants. He was shocked by my undiplomatic elaboration, but as he processed my comments, he looked at me in a way that made me feel as if he could understand my reasoning and motivation. He wondered about my openness towards Father Teo and I explained to him that Father Teo was not about religion, he was about spirituality. He seemed to have an a-ha experience.

14 UNIVERSAL LIFE: MY NEW PLANT

When I returned to school as a PhD student, I felt compelled to confess to my advisor that I was in urgent need of improving my statistics and so I boldly asked him if he could give me a group of students for a research project. The truth is often the most shocking thing and no matter how honest you are some people just don't believe you. My advisor had difficulties accepting the idea that after many years out of formal training, I had forgotten many concepts and on top of that I had never learned certain concepts at all. Be it as it was, statistics was not the only bonding experience with my professor.

Once I had my group of students, I gained access to the privileged PhD room and more than that to the sanctuary of the conference room of our department. After the meeting of all the PhD students regarding their new projects, I could not resist questioning the professor on the state of the plants in the conference room. He looked at me as if he had just been given a magical magnifying glass.

Since he had some difficulties understanding standard human language without any statistical complications, I explained myself in no uncertain terms. "Not that I would expect YOU to water the plants in the conference room, but doesn't at least the cleaning lady...?"

He interrupted me abruptly before I could finish and in a shocked way he only answered: "No, nobody does."

"Then from now on I declare myself in charge of watering the plants around here." He must have been at a perfect loss because he had no idea what to say or do, he only stood around glued to the ground like a statue. I did not mean to put him into the same comatose state that the plants were in.

And within the quietness of my own mind, I could not resist asking if by the end of my scientific project I was going to be just as brain-dead as all the other humans around, with the only exception of knowing more about statistics than before. If the unspoken deal was that I could only learn statistics by watching some innocent plants die, then that was an unacceptable offer for me. In my opinion one can learn plenty of statistics and water all plants adequately. Why that was a contradiction in our department, I will never know.

After a few minutes the professor could speak again and asked me, "What do you plan to do?" – as if that was not obvious. I looked at him to express my surprise that I even had to answer such a question, but since I was in the scientific mode I elaborated on the trivial fact that the plants were in urgent need of watering by adding that I was going to buy new soil and a bottle of plant nourishment the following day.

He seemed pleased and wanted to leave the room, but after making one step towards the door, he came back, pointed towards one of the plants and stated, "This one we will throw into the trash!"

I was outraged and countered.

"But it is still alive!"

He would not let go and said, "But it looks so ugly."

Now I was at my personal limit of putting up with nonsense and angrily said, "You people around here! Not only did you make sure that these plants are no beauties, but after letting them die you even want to throw this one away while it is still alive!"

"But!" he tried to say, which I cut short.

"No but!"

I suppose no human being had ever spoken to him that way, let alone a student. Student or not, or professor or not, universal laws are valid for all of us, also in Vienna! He left the room without saying a word.

Little did I know what was going to happen within the next few hours. I came back to the conference room and found the designated plant in the trash!! While I was ready to explode, the unfortunate man also came into the conference room and I could only confront him with the following. "What is this?"

Had I been his wife and had I caught him with his pants down, he could not have looked guiltier. The expression on his face was a combination between Machiavelli and Uriah Heep (from *David Copperfield* by Charles Dickens, not the music group).

He only said, "Because it is so ugly, I do not want this plant in the conference room!"

All of a sudden? The whole department must have spent months watching the plants in a coma, not caring about their beauty or lack thereof, and not even caring about their survival.

"I told you not to throw away the plant. I will take care of it and I have no ambition to have the plant win a beauty contest."

He was really surprised how determined I was.

"You are not going to take it out of the trash can?"

"Don't you worry about that!" I said in an unfriendly tone.

He felt he had won. Of course, I grabbed the poor plant out of the trash and took it to my PhD room.

The following day as I had already said, I brought in fresh soil and a bottle of plant nourishment. I spent hours taking care of the old plants and also saving the poor little guy who had been sentenced to death by the professor.

The professor came back to the conference room to check on what I was doing. Once he discovered the bottle of plant nourishment, he said, "This will stay in my office!" and grabbed the bottle.

I asked him, following him to his office, "How do you imagine that I can take care of all the plants if you keep the plant nourishment in your office?" He seemed to have a brilliant idea. "You can come into my office anytime you want." I tried to stay as rational as I could.

"But you have meetings all the time! Why would I ever want to disturb you?"

The apparently triumphant only stated, "This bottle stays in my office!"

"That is OK with me!" I replied, which he mistook as a declaration of submissiveness. But my inner geisha was on vacation. "But since your suggestion does not really work for me, I will buy myself another bottle of plant nourishment."

He stood there in the middle of his office with his mouth open and shocked. To make myself clear I continued, "First thing early tomorrow morning!"

I have never witnessed anyone lose a battle of words with such a devastating effect as the professor. I really felt like screaming, "You see? This is why things go wrong in the world! People don't know the difference between correlation and causality!" However, I stopped myself in my tracks because I did not want him to think I was playing the statistical smart ass on him.

Said and done, the following morning I bought myself my own bottle of plant nourishment and put it on the windowsill next to my desk in the PhD room. While I was working on the computer having forgotten the entire interaction regarding the plants, the professor came in and in an ironic tone asked, "Well, where is your bottle?"

Torn away from my science I asked myself, "Bottle of what?" having lost track of our earlier conversation.

Coming back to reality, I only pointed at the bottle on my windowsill. He seemed unhappy. Why two grown-ups should share a bottle of plant nourishment when it is inconvenient from a practical perspective, I will never understand. The professor became even unhappier when he found THE plant on my desk in a new pot and with new soil. He did not even start a discussion about it because he had understood that I was going to defend life in all its universal forms.

To make sure my comatose plant was in a positive healing process, I wrote a note saying "I love you just the way you are!" and glued it to the bottom of the pot. I telepathically explained to my plant that we could not afford to have the note placed visibly on the pot, but that under the pot nobody would care to check. The plant must have been quite happy with me because it recovered day by day and became one of the most beautiful plants I ever saw. It survived for many more years and I am very happy that I was a part of its life.

15 "KARMA OR NOT, I AM THE WOMAN ON TOP OF YOU!"

As our building was renovated, many apartments stood empty for a while, but after a number of years of renovation ordeal, new people started moving in. I was partially quite curious who would be my new neighbors from the surrounding empty apartments. One day I noticed that the apartment from under my room had beautiful new red curtains hanging and, of course, I was curious to see who the new inhabitant was.

A few days later, as I went to bed in the evening I heard loud and exotic music and I figured it came from downstairs. For the whole night this unusual music did not stop. I could not identify the origin of the music, but I thought it came from around China or India. Needless to say, I had a sleepless night and felt very tired the following day. I am used to sleeping in the dark and can only relax when everything is quiet.

Shortly after I met someone in the building who I thought had to be one of the new neighbors. I asked him if he by any chance was my new neighbor from the apartment with the red curtains. And when he answered in the affirmative, I introduced myself. "I am the woman on top of you!" He was a bit surprised, but we shook hands and I welcomed him to our building.

As we were about to part, I asked him if he had celebrated a party a couple of nights before. He said yes and wondered how I knew. I told him I had heard his exotic music the whole night. He explained that he would have such a party once a year. I asked him what his name was and he introduced himself as Karma. I told him, "Karma, when your party comes around next year, please let me know when you plan to celebrate." Karma looked at me as if I was joking, but promised to do so nonetheless.

What Karma could not have known at that point was that architecturally I shared my room with him as it was on top of his, but there were two other rooms in my apartment I could escape to for the next party. Karma shared one room with me and one room with my next door neighbor, an older lady. Just before we parted I asked Karma where he was from. "Tibet."

"That's why your music sounded so exotic to my ears". I left him with the statement "Great to have you around, Karma from Tibet, and we will talk more next time we bump into each other in the building."

A while later, my next door neighbor told me about the wonderful massage Karma gave her and wanted to know if I had also received one already. I had never seen my neighbor so excited before and at that point we had been next door neighbors for about 25 years. With the neighbor's enthusiastic recommendation, I asked Karma if I could also have one because I was curious about his work. When the time for my appointment came I was more than ready for relaxation. And when I entered

Karma's apartment I knew I was in another world. To me it was like entering a temple, in a different time, in a different space. I told him, "Karma, you are coming from a very special place!"

Karma was flattered and while I was admiring the entire decoration, the crystals and the pictures on the wall, he added, "I am coming directly from the Dalai Lama!" I had never heard someone be more proud about his origin than Karma at that moment. But the first time I met Karma in the building, I had already noticed his special energy and I immediately made up my mind that I could only like a person like him. Dalai Lama or not, Karma could not have increased in my high regard for him.

The massage was a most wonderful and mystical experience for many reasons, even a funny one, as I got a chance to listen to the same exotic music again that I had heard during the night of his party. I could only agree with the next door neighbor that Karma's work had a unique touch to it and I knew I would be back again.

After several of his massages, I told him "Karma, you might think me arrogant, but I feel you moved into this building just for me!" Karma laughed, but he understood what I meant. With the passing of time, Karma told me about his family and his friends from Tibet. When one of his doctor friends from Tibet came to visit, I also got a chance to speak to him. I could only marvel at the ancient wisdom of their alternative medicine. I could only wonder why Western medicine had such a different approach and declared many many medical conditions as incurable while for medical systems coming from ancient cultures everything had a solution.

I came to the conclusion that Western medicine is linear while Eastern medicine is holistic. The Western world defines as real "I only believe what I see," while the

Eastern world defines as real "I only see what I believe". Why is there no crossover in these two approaches? Why do we have to have the one or the other? And why do we prefer to make ourselves dependent on technology beyond the level of rationality and common sense? Why do we prefer to be determined and defined by the visible while we fully neglect the invisible?

Karma received friends and family from Tibet on a regular basis and I found out that maybe even the Dalai Lama could come one day. I remember when hearing this that I thought to myself, "Please divinity, when the Dalai Lama comes, let the next door neighbor be the woman on top of him!"

16 MY NATIVE AMERICAN SHAMAN

When I was a little girl my brother who is only a bit younger than me used to love playing cowboys and Indians. I am not even sure if that is the name of the game, but it was about cowboys and Indians fighting and killing each other. I remember that when a horse with an Indian dropped dead, I immediately came to pick it up and bring it back to life. I have no idea why I did that I only remember doing it.

As a little girl I did not know anything about Native Americans, except when they showed up in American movies, especially in Westerns. In school my history books did not make any particular mention of Native Americans. Only years later when as a young adult alternative medicine was conquering my life, did the Native Americans reenter my consciousness along with the Chinese and the Indians. Traditional Chinese Medicine and Ayurveda are closely related to the Native American healing art. Everything alternative fascinated me from homeopathy to spagyrics and everything in between.

For a number of months, I had felt that it was time to choose a Native American shaman and make contact. However, things on an everyday basis kept me so busy that I postponed my concrete decision of making a choice. Within me I felt a growing desire to have my own Native American shaman and struggled through the chores of everyday life before I finally finished my research and felt I found the right person for me.

In Europe it was early in the morning, but in America it was past eleven at night when my soul said that "I have to call now". Usually, I follow this guidance without any reservation. In this case I did not want to appear impolite on our very first contact. The information came again to "call now" and so finally I did. I was prepared for something else, but not for what truly happened.

I introduced myself by name and geographic location. At the other end of the line, in the softest and mildest tone a motherly voice said, "My god, I am so happy to finally hear from you!!"

I was speechless and did not know how to react.

My Native American shaman explained: "I was informed about you by my guides about six months ago. I kept wondering what took you so long?"

I had never been more surprised in my entire life. At the other end of the world somebody knew I was going to call and was so happy to finally hear from me!

I tried my best to stay as composed as possible and explain my story in the most rational way. My Native American shaman knew how to listen, knew what to say and also knew how to say it. I had never experienced someone so much in tune with me as I experienced her to be.

Our conversation moved according to a special energetic pattern which was completely beyond the usual human sphere. Even after our discussion I continued feeling her presence and I was very touched by her wisdom, gentleness, caring and talent. My shaman accompanied me through the day and it was such a pleasure to feel her aura around me practically at all times. It was a most amazing experience staying in touch with her. Our contact had something celestial about it which I cannot put into words. All her suggestions made sense both energetically and pragmatically. She was grounded and etheric at the same time. I don't know how she managed to keep the balance, but she was 100% in balance.

As I pondered about her, I felt put into another galaxy in which spiritual laws finally get manifested. There was something very familiar about this new galaxy, but there was also the awareness that we humans have difficulties staying aligned with it. All her recommendations made me have mystical experiences which transformed some of my older views on things into new expanded insights. As I look back at my experience with my Native American shaman, I wonder how come their knowledge has so far not been integrated to a higher degree and on a grander scale. Why has our world not discovered the treasures that lie within the Native American heritage? Why are they so marginalized at a time when union and togetherness define the pulse of time?

The profound power of the Native American frequency has been available to us for such a long time while we either ignored it or neglected it. I cannot wait to join one of the retreat groups led by my Native American shaman and benefit from the immense spiritual potential as a human and as a soul.

17 SISTER AUGUSTIA

As I was lying in my bed relaxing after my session of physiotherapy at the clinic, I heard a knock on my door and as I looked up a Roman Catholic nun stood in front of me. Her energy told me that she had completely transcended being a nun and being a Roman Catholic. She asked me about my roommate whom she apparently came to visit. I explained to her that Dana was in one of her sessions, but that I would let her know about the visitor. She said, "Please tell her Sister Augustia wanted to see her!"

I promised to do so and the nun was again on her way out, but after making a few steps, she came back and asked me, "Do you also need to talk to me?"

Under no circumstances would I agree to, first, making myself dependent on a dialogue with a Roman Catholic nun, but second, to being impolite to someone just because of their faith. So I answered.

"I am in no need to talk to you, but I would enjoy making the choice of wanting to talk to you if you have a few minutes for me!"

She looked very surprised, but accepted my answer and

came closer to me.

I was in no need to talk to a Roman Catholic nun, but I definitely wanted to talk to someone with the energies of Sister Augustia. She wanted to know why I needed physiotherapy at that point and how I was doing in general. She gave me some of the usual slogans that people hear and I explained to her that I was past that level.

She was very happy to hear that, because afterwards everything we said to one another was full of life, spontaneity and depth. Sister Augustia came across to me as one of the very few people who had integrated their inner shadow. She was a truly knowing soul. I was surprised to find someone of her consciousness within the Roman Catholic Church. I am not saying that these souls do not exist there, but usually what people say sounds more like brainwashing than anything else. I had the most wonderful time talking to Sister Augustia. I always enjoyed her visits and I found it very healing to share with her some of my thoughts while she listened and offered me her profound insights. The way she talked, the tone of her voice carried a deep sense of solace. Her eyes communicated the fact that she was completely in her center having integrated the polarities. Also her aura was a proof of her conscious connection with divinity. I was impressed by the way she was connected to the flow of energies. Usually I had observed this connection only in people who had practiced something like yoga or tai chi for a significant number of years.

How Sister Augustia got to this high level, I cannot say, but I know she touched me deeply. I have the impression not only that she had this high level, but also that she was fully aware of it. Sometimes I come across highly developed souls who are not aware of it. Sister Augustia was both highly developed and fully aware of it. Sister

Augustia was much more than what she presented at face value. I understood that everybody enjoyed speaking to her and appreciated her qualities. Actually, to me she represented the opposite of what I know to be a Germanic Roman Catholic. While I would expect fear, denial and punishment to accompany every thought of a Germanic Roman Catholic, Sister Augustia was amazingly free of all three of them. Due to the fact that physically I was not very fit, I interacted with Sister Augustia on a very superficial level according to my own standard. I found it a true pity that I could not do more, but that was the reality of our context together. I hope one day to have a chance to talk to Sister Augustia again and share with her our experiences that connect us to our source.

In my memory, Sister Augustia was a most remarkable soul who grounded her divine nature by everything she did. I think Sister Augustia could only have such a positive impact on me because she allowed herself two things which actually never happen to a Roman Catholic. First, she allowed herself inner freedom, and second, she gave herself permission for self-empowerment. Germanic Roman Catholics are defined by their immense fear of hell and a constant expectation that no matter what, they eventually end up there. On the human side it is both ridiculous and embarrassing to listen to a Roman Catholic grown-up share these fears, but on the spiritual side it is devastating to observe the negative effect these fears produce. And self-empowerment is non-existent to a Germanic Roman Catholic. They have never heard of it, they don't know what it is and they don't practice it. They are determined by the external definition of some outer source that claims all the power only to misuse it.

I wondered if within Christianity the Roman Catholic Church is so out of touch simply because it is the oldest. Or is the truth not connected just to age and time, but to major manipulations of information and concepts?

I also wondered as I got to know Sister Augustia a bit better if the first and only female pope in the history of humankind was of a similar caliber to her?

18 BERKIN: "A MOST MODERN MOM!"

My daughter's phone rang and from her answer I gathered the person at the end of the line must have asked what she was doing at that moment. "I am sitting in my mother's room chatting to her."

It was Berkin, one of my daughter's friends from Turkey. Even though Berkin was not present, whenever he is on the phone we laugh a lot and philosophize about different things in life. He wanted to know what our plans were for the next few hours, probably because he wanted to meet my daughter downtown.

"I am waiting for *The Girls at the Playboy Mansion* to start on *E!Entertainment*," I stated for my part.

Berkin at the other end of the line heard me and burst out in laughter, "A most modern mom!"

My daughter was a bit shocked and wanted to know what happens in this show. I explained to her and Berkin that *The Girls at the Playboy Mansion* was not on the *The Plaboy Channel* and that there was nothing explicitly sexual about these episodes.

The two younger ones wanted to know what the episodes were about. I explained to them that I had only seen a few and the most memorable ones were about the party where everybody dressed up as Disney cartoon characters. But there were also the ones about the little doggy who wanted to become a TV commercial star and needed training, or the little unhappy bird with a trauma from one of his past lives who needed reincarnation therapy. The most moving one was about them visiting the young soldiers who would soon leave for the war in Iraq. In the most unexpected episode, the girls ended up in prison while visiting Prince Albert in Monte Carlo, even though the purpose of their visit was to receive an accolade for their show.

"Don't they have sex?" my daughter asked.

"Not in front of the camera!" I said. "But otherwise I truly hope they all do!"

Berkin could not stop laughing while my daughter pretended to be surprised at my answer. I wondered at that point why my daughter at 16 had not been able to escape the usual brainwashing regarding social sexual mores and attitudes.

As a mom I felt like a complete failure in my conscious attempts to teach her to at least feel comfortable talking about sex, of course with the higher aim of enabling her one day to have sex without the usual guilt, inhibitions and complications that mainstream upbringing causes in all children, especially girls.

I remember the day when she was in third grade and I told her, "Tomorrow night they are showing a movie on television which I would like us to watch together and if you feel too tired after our TV night, you do not have to go to school the following morning." She was a bit surprised, but accepted my statement without any comments. The following night she was ready and looked very puzzled as I told her, "Just one thing, darling! Try not to laugh too hard when the funny scenes come because we do not want to wake up grandma and grandpa. They would not understand."

My daughter moved through the movie having lots of fun and plenty of insights which she was not able to share with me immediately. I knew she was processing information on a deeper level than was customary for an eight-year-old. The movie we watched that night was *When Harry Met Sally...* Needless to say, the movie energized her so much that she said at the end of it, "Mommy, I can go to school tomorrow. Wake me up!" And with the sunniest face ever, she moved into her bed that night.

I would have never have dared to recommend her *When Harry Met Sally...*, had it not been for her inquisitiveness at the age of four and a half. One hot summer evening, while I was torturing myself by ironing some laundry, one of the German channels showed a program about sexual emancipation in the 70's. My daughter moved from a lying position to sitting up as if she had heard the news of the century. I can imagine at four and a half it was. She looked hypnotized. I could only ask her, "Are you interested?" Still glued to the screen, she nodded.

"Then listen well!"

She did.

The then already twenty-year old movie that was to emancipate generations of Germans could not have been more childish, more ridiculous, or more embarrassing to every liberated human. But for a four-and-a-half-year-old girl it was apparently fascinating. She could not get enough of it.

During the commercial break, I asked her "What is sex?" She looked at me as if I was the most stupid person in the world. She was right. I behaved in the most stupid way.

She looked at me and asked, "But mommy, do you not know?" She didn't wait for my answer, but only replied, "Sex is flowers and champagne."

I had never heard a more innocent explanation of sex before or after as a matter of fact. I was so surprised that I spontaneously asked, "What do you mean?"

She was outraged at my stupidity and must have wondered how I managed to become a mom in the first place. "But mommy, do you not know? He comes and brings flowers and champagne and then they kiss."

That conversation with my four-and-a-half-year-old was most enlightening to me. I was happy about her intuitive approach to sexual matters and her natural disposition to talk freely about it. Grown-ups, if they ever had it, lose their intuition and natural inclination when it comes to sexual topics.

When I went back to school years later, during a lunch break, a colleague of mine asked me if I had already watched the new series. I had not watched television in years due to being very busy and I asked her what new series she was talking about. She could only offer "These women talking..." That was not really enough for me to know what she meant and so I asked her about the title: *Sex and the City*. I had never even heard of it, let alone watched it. But apparently my grown-up colleague felt too embarrassed to elaborate and so we left it at that.

Lucky me my daughter was about ten at this time and she was the one who would save me from my ignorance. She came to me one night and said, "I think I will go to bed very late again tonight, because there is something on television I need to watch."

I noticed in her voice that it must have been about more than just going to bed late, because honestly that was already her habit at that point and she had my permission. So I asked her what was so important to her about that night.

"I'm watching *Sex and the City*," she said. Remembering my incomplete conversation with my colleague from a short while ago, I asked her what it was all about.

"Mommy, it is all about sex!!"

I was impressed by the child's power of synthesis compared to the adult woman's uneasiness about the series.

"Do you like it?"

She nodded vigorously.

"Do you learn a lot from it?"

She nodded again just as vigorously.

"Then make sure you watch it every time!"

She looked very liberated all of a sudden and I understood she was looking for my permission to enjoy seeing the show. I wondered what happened in the course of time to the four-year-old who could still enjoy Harry and Sally at eight, but felt she was doing something wrong at ten when watching *Sex and the City*.

Two years later, I also had a chance to watch *Sex and the City* for the very first time. Too bad that my daughter was on vacation at that time and we could not share the experience of finally meeting her sex teachers!! When she came back, we talked about the series and I felt that I was catching up with something that my daughter had wanted to share with me much earlier.

As a child like her, with her experiences at four, eight and ten, and with a mom like me, I truly could not understand why at 16 hearing about my enjoyment of watching *The Girls at the Playboy Mansion* could shock her so much. I knew her reaction had nothing to do with Berkin, but with the general constellation of our society that preaches a form of self-sabotage in connection to human sexuality.

Now, I have no idea about the girls who live at the Playboy Mansion and their religion or spirituality. I never heard any explicit references in the show. What I can say is that they are very kind human beings, very grounded, very centered, very realistic, and at the same time very free and at peace with themselves and the world around them. This is a lot more than I can say about the so-called normal person, who is tormented by conventions and traditions which are then used to pass judgment about others. Even though I do not share the sexual philosophy of the girls at the Playboy Mansion, I know they would never pass judgment on me just as I would never pass judgment on them.

No matter that Berkin found me to be "a most modern mom", I am sad to observe how even the most liberal upbringing is threatened to be destroyed by a world full of misunderstanding when it comes to sexuality. *The Feminine Mystique* appears to be in need of an update for each new generation!

19 BURAK AND THE HAJJ

"Mom, let me introduce you to my new friend Burak!" my teenage daughter said while she brought the young man into my room. I extended my hand towards him and welcomed him to our home. He didn't expect to be treated politely which made me very sad. My sadness and his insecurity served as a valuable hint of the delicate situations humans find themselves in when they focus on differences instead of similarities.

I asked Burak where he was from.
He answered in the most apologetic way, "Turkey."
I continued. "Then you must be a Muslim!"
Burak moved from apologetic to guilty, and I countered. "You are just the person I was waiting for!"
Burak and my daughter thought I was crazy. But congruent as I am, within seconds they knew what I was after.
"I watched all the presentations of Hajj on *CNN*."
Burak lightened up like the sun. I needed to ask Burak about where the Hajj was taking place. He was not sure what to answer and I explained that I thought it should be

Mekka. He confirmed this and I wondered why they never mentioned Mekka on *CNN*.

I had spent the entire day being impressed by the huge masses of people participating in the pilgrimage and by the extremely high frequency of the energy of the masses. In an interview a lady expressed her gratitude for her big chance to be there and her hopes for having enough money in the future to be able to return.

"Burak, how expensive is it to go to Mekka?"

Burak was too confused to know, but in his eyes I saw curiosity in regards to my question.

I lectured him, "Look Burak, going to Mekka should not be a question of money. How could this nice woman ever be worried about having enough money in the future to return?"

As always poor Burak did not know what to say. I continued with my lecture. "You know Burak, the Arab countries are some of the richest in the world and I recommend they create a fund to help people in need finance their pilgrimage to Mekka. It is wonderful when people want to be close to god and we need to take money out of the equation!"

Burak was too shocked to answer.

"When are you planning to go to Mekka, Burak?" I asked.

From his facial expression I could see that he had no such plans for a long time. Burak only uttered, "When I am older."

And I countered, "Burak, you should go when you are younger, not older!"

"But people don't go when they are young."

"Why? Because it is too expensive?"

Burak was not sure.

I wanted to know if I could also go to Mekka or whether this was again one of the things I would be rejected from because I had the wrong religion? Burak really did not know.

It must have been for the very first time in his life that he heard a non-Muslim interested in joining the pilgrimage.

"The atmosphere is so nice that I also want to be in the middle of it!" I explained.

Burak was completely surprised, but could not be of any help with the information I wanted. What Burak could not have known was that on top of being impressed by the event of Hajj, watching it on television reconnected me to the same feeling of peace and clarity I had had while reading the Koran in my mid-twenties in order to satisfy my own curiosity about the variety of religions. I was more than surprised to discover the story of Jesus and his family in the Koran and the bits and pieces of text I read confirmed to me that it was as similar in philosophy and purpose as I had found the Bible and the teachings of Buddha to be.

It is too bad that in the German-speaking countries people coming from Turkey or other Muslim countries do not experience openness and appreciation on a regular basis. As Europeans we tend to think that Muslim men lost their power to feel because they are traditional and Muslim women lost their power to think because they wear a hijab on their heads.

While watching the people at Mekka, I did not think for a second that they were unfeeling or unthinking. It makes me very sad when prejudice overpowers reality. I experienced the people interviewed as being good-hearted, well-intentioned and highly intelligent. They were the kind of people I wish I could have as my friends. There was nothing unfamiliar or strange about them. Quite the contrary, I was happy about the sense of innocence, centeredness and balance they displayed. They reminded me of my two special Muslim friends Esma and Azita.

At some point my daughter interrupted my conversation with Burak, probably feeling that I was monopolizing the discussion beyond politeness. I was happy to hear Burak talk to her in a fluent way once they left my room, because he had been a practicing mute there. Good to see that I had not done any harm to Burak by being curious or inquisitive about his culture. Burak must have been surprised that he was welcomed by me with all his differences, especially in the year 2009. He made me aware of how much healing we all need!

20 APPLYING THE ENERGIES OF OUR TIME

Where do we go from here? And HOW do we go from here?

The energies of our time are new. That might sound like the most ridiculous statement ever simply because all ages can claim the same of their own times. When I refer to "new" I mean on the energetic level. In the past "new" usually referred to the social or economic or political or technological levels.

It is not easy to make myself understood by touching on a subject that probably most people are not aware of on the conscious level. I can though very well imagine that most people are aware of it on the pre-conscious level. Most of us move through life making our own observations and gaining our own insights, but at times we experience difficulties putting these observations and these insights into their categories. We have all noticed that things done by us in familiar ways do not produce the same results that we would expect according to old patterns. This is due to the fact that the energies of our time are increasingly non-linear, holistic, lightful and non-dominant.

Non-linear means that if we want to experience the world based only on logic and sequential thinking, we will not succeed. Holistic means that we need to simultaneously integrate our thinking and our feeling in order to behave in balance and harmony. Lightful means that the universe provides an energy that brings everything to the surface and makes it visible to an extent that nothing stays in the hidden or in the obscure, displaying all manipulative or abusive behaviors. Non-dominant refers to actions based on interactions rooted in the awareness of interdependence.

It is remarkable to notice that throughout the entire evolutionary process of humankind, the new energies were present, but only in the area of the arts. All artistic manifestations are generated and sustained by the energies we experience in our time to take over all aspects of life.

In the past, only artists got away with displaying their connection to what otherwise could have become either socially, economically, or politically undesirable. Arts were the only holistic expression of the past. It is ironic that to this day we think of artists as starving and recommend our children, "First go and learn something meaningful to make money," before we encourage them to pick up a brush, play the guitar, start singing or make a movie! The arts have stayed marginalized even though they did have a certain function in our world. It is even more ironic that energetically speaking the arts represent the only existing bridge between the past and the future. The saying "passing the test of time" is an indication that humanity has always allowed the existence of what we today call the new energies. The new energies are about transcending the hold of time on our reality by integrating all experiences into one form and becoming artists of life instead of artisans.

Some of the most famous works of art embody the fascinating energies that humanity is experiencing in our time beyond the area of the arts. The new energies of our time are about expanding what we already know from the arts to every aspect of human interaction. We can ask ourselves, "Is what I am doing here able to pass the test of time?" If the answer is yes, then we are mastering the task well.

A lot more could be said about the new energies of our time, but I hope the main characteristics offer a practical overview. On the pre-conscious level all the characteristics are known to most of us, but now that we have categories, our knowledge can move from the pre-conscious to the conscious level. Maybe all of a sudden personal observations and insights make perfect sense and fall into their right place.

In order to clarify the point, I would also like to mention the main characteristics of the old times and their energies: coercion of the less powerful by the more powerful, dependence of the less powerful on the more powerful, polarized phenomena in which the positive goes to a very small percentage while the negative goes to the larger percentage, criteria used for such phenomena based on demographics as the source of prejudice. Dominance and exploitation are accompanied also by fragmentation which hinders humans in achieving the feeling that they have the overview. Very often un-clarity or even chaos can result. Fragmentation undermines the ability to have control over a process and can easily lead into powerlessness. On top of that, only superficial interactions are possible.

Due to the old pattern, humanity has become over-thinking and under-feeling. We are completely out of balance regarding both aspects because our thinking is usually more a form of "thinking that we think" while our feelings usually become manifested in some form of mass hysteria or mass psychosis.

Put in very scary terms, "old" versus "new" is about male versus female energies! The truth is, it is not really about male versus female. It is more about the male energy as applied due to human misunderstandings, which I call the deformed male energies, versus female energies as provided by the evolutionary force. These have a dynamic of their own. They have not yet been understood and thus also not yet been applied in a misunderstood way. The male in its misunderstood forms is very superficial while the female as offered by the universe is remarkably profound. Since our functioning has traditionally been very superficial, being confronted with phenomena based on female energies throw us into personal, national, international crises in all aspects of our human life.

To make sure I present my thoughts clearly I would like to provide here a short summary which includes all the aspects I just mentioned in the paragraph above.

Summary

1. Pure male energies:
Provided by the universe throughout humankind's history.
Expressed extremely rarely among humans.
The ideal pure male energy corresponds to the Chinese term of Yang and all its characteristics and qualities.

2. Deformed male energies:
Male energies misconceptualized by humans.

Applied in a deformed way.

Dominant instead of cooperative.

The typical male expression throughout the ages.

3. Pure female energies:

Provided by the universe throughout humankind's history.

Expressed naturally by most women but neglected, ignored or punished by men.

Causes fear and insecurity in men, forcing them to suppress and control it.

The ideal pure female energy corresponds to the Chinese term of Yin and all its characteristics and qualities.

We women are made to think there is something wrong with our pure female energies because men react so inadequately to them.

We women may learn thanks to the help of the new energies that our pure female energies are unique, irreplaceable and invincible, independent or other people's misinterpretations or wishes.

4. Deformed female energies:

In danger of becoming understood but misapplied.

Rarely expressed by women.

As we women as a group become more powerful, there is the risk of thinking that we have to be the better men.

I need to question here if the phenomenon of emancipation has been used to enable us to become better women, or just better men.

I hope this summary clarifies my points and puts things into perspective.

Even though I haven't read it yet, the book *Women Should Rule the World* seems to be about the application of the new energies of our time. Just from the title I know I would enjoy the book without reservation. And now I even have good news for all of us: since the new energies are all female, we can rest assured not only that women should rule the world, but that women indeed rule the world!

Another interesting aspect of our current situation is that again and again we hear vague comments that imply the female energies, but the expression of the people commenting on them are so abstract that they seem to be identified as such only by the initiated. If we want to heal ourselves and our world, either all of us turn into initiated people or we make our expressions more concrete for every human being to understand. Otherwise humanity stays caught on the pre-conscious level and wastes valuable resources that could be put to better use when acting from the conscious level instead of from the pre-conscious.

The new energies have nothing to do with esoteric concepts. Much too often such concepts lack grounding and at the same time do not facilitate a stronger connection to our souls. People often claim how much they would like to be more intuitive and sometimes people even aspire to being able to talk to angels. Lacking grounding and missing the connection with the soul hinders the development of all psychic abilities. The new energies effortlessly facilitate such a development under the conditions that we focus on - staying grounded and connecting to our soul. No artificial methods are necessary. We are finally able to transcend esoteric phenomena.

One of the unwritten rules of the old pattern is that some of us are more deserving than others. We are all just as deserving, the only criterion of differentiation being our level of consciousness. The old pattern would use criteria that only discriminate.

The original state of creation was defined as consisting

of the following elements: harmony, joy, effortlessness, awareness, peace, balance, transcendence, insight, intelligence, prosperity, and success. From among all these elements, the energy of our time indicates the heightened significance of "intelligence". Creation is an act of intelligence on the part of an intelligent creator. We could also say creation is divine art, but the question is why does it look more as if the art has an "f" in front of it? The humans react with, "Oh, how shocking!" while the universe has a good laugh.

From all characteristics of divinity, humanity is lagging behind especially in the area of intelligence even though science has always proudly proclaimed that it is our intelligence that differentiates us from the animals. How ironic! Maybe it is fair to say that we have a wonderful latent potential for intelligence, but have not yet bothered to apply it on a profound level! But lucky us, the energies of our time are kicking us in all the right places and we finally get a chance to do what we were supposed to do from the beginning of times!

If we don't act upon this chance now, spiritual pain would not only continue to be humanity's only state, but it will become increasingly unbearable. We do have a choice! We always did. It is up to us to act in a way that facilitates healing both personally and globally. That critical mass which is always needed to trigger a change has long been reached. Regarding the energies of our time, the critical mass only needs to make one step from the pre-conscious to the conscious level and instantly all aspects of our life have a new dimension and meaning.

Now, a few words to the concept of "cause and effect". Some people might think that only after having numerous mystical experiences, can they or may wake up to their innate spiritual potential. The truth is if we believe in "cause and effect", it works the other way around. First waking up to our innate spiritual potential facilitates numerous mystical experiences.

It is most unfortunate that according to the old pattern human intelligence, due to its rudimentary development, decided to hold on to the past instead of realizing that constant co-creation is the purpose of life. Forcing ourselves to imitate the past robs us of our spiritual potential and hinders us in becoming true expressions of divinity. Forcing ourselves to imitate the past only creates conflicts.

It is also most unfortunate that when in the past spiritual people transcended the concept of pushing themselves to imitate the past they were misinterpreted as saints or something akin to that. All they were doing was to manifest their spiritual potential as true expressions of divinity. Human misunderstanding threw humanity into deeper trouble instead of using intelligence to understand these exceptional people and letting their behavior serve as a model to others. That's how religiosity dominated the human body and the human mind creating a catch twenty-two situation in which the "truth" or "reality" was presented in a certain light, even though the situation was the exact opposite! Telling people to hold on to the past, while they actually needed to transcend the past in order to be spiritually free, was the biggest pitfall in the history of humankind. Buddha apparently said, "The only constant in life is change!" Why humanity has failed to understood Buddha's message is an enigma. Apparently not even one of humanity's greatest avatars managed to get the message across!

According to the energies of our time, all misunderstandings are surfacing more and more and at the same time they get disempowered. Spirituality implies applying eternal universal principles to life as it happens in the moment. Imitation is not only wrong, it is fatal. It keeps humanity separated from the source and it perpetuates spiritual pain.

For us humans in order to connect to divine intelligence, it is important to find grounding methods to also be intelligent. Once we learn to practice "grounded intelligence", spiritual pain will start diminishing until one day it can completely disappear from human experience. Actually, the second humans start practicing "grounded intelligence" the reality of our life changes completely for the better. Due to all the misunderstandings the majority of us assume that first we have to get into some special state in order to be close to divinity. All these measures prove to be artificial if they don't carry within themselves the frequency of groundedness. Every single human act can carry within it a divine spark, even the simplest one.

It is not to say that "grounded intelligence" as a reflection of the divine spark within humans is easy to be achieved. "Grounded intelligence" presupposes that humans are willing to interact with all aspects of any given task on the most profound level. When acting in a way that is in line "grounded intelligence", one has the experience that the energy goes down right to the center of the earth. Nothing else could be done more or better. Every experience accompanied by such a phenomenon is highly spiritual. The majority of humanity is far away from such an application. However, I can name a few examples that show that it is possible to experience "grounded intelligence" on an everyday basis. All of the people involved are spiritual - maybe not necessarily on the conscious level - but they are expressing that spark of divinity and are enabling the manifestation of that original state of creation, whether they know it or not and if they like it or not.

"NOT RELIGIOUS, SPIRITUAL!"
A HOLISTIC JOURNEY BEYOND TIME AND SPACE

I can well imagine that the examples I will present will produce very polarized reactions. According to the old pattern criticism may come from the powerless that swim in bitterness and cynicism, while those at the other end of the spectrum will gain new unexpected insights. Of course, I moved through life trying to connect to all expressions of divine sparks.

Before I give specific examples I'd like to mention that even within academic research there are hints that scientists are slowly becoming aware of the new energies in the form of what they call "post-modernism". Especially the disciplines of economics, sociology, medicine, and physics have impressed me with their new perspectives on how humans interact and how they influence the manifestation of matter. Quantum physics is regarded as the science closest to divine consciousness. In the recent past, quantum physics has become the scientific foundation of many alternative methods in medicine. Sociology is also contributing new insights, especially when it looks at processes such as leadership. Economics has long transcended both *homo economicus* and *homo psychologicus*.

If quantum physics is capable of discovering our holographic universe, if medicine is capable of finding healing, if sociology is capable of addressing our uniqueness within society's conglomeration, if economics is able to tune into our nature as beyond the psychological layer, then we can fully trust that every human being has the potential of applying the new energies of our time, starting with the concept of "grounded intelligence". In case academe still appears caught in the ivory tower, it is best to look at the new energies from a pragmatic point of view. The scientific post-modernism may have a face and even a name!

One example to which most people might have access to around the globe is *CNN*. It truly brings the world together! Considering the fact that we are talking about people working, "simply" doing their jobs on an everyday basis might startle some when presented as an expression of spirituality. I have marveled over the years at the fact that everyone working for *CNN* is a living example of "grounded intelligence", displaying maximum willingness to deal with all aspects of any given task on the most profound level. The entire world is a better place because of *CNN* and the way people work there. The truth is we are not only dealing with people at work, but with souls at work! They bring in their uniqueness in the most natural way. If they know it or not, they fulfill the most healing function for our planet. I once heard that when humans are doing the right thing, a gong can be heard in the universe. I can add to that that each time *CNN* gets active, another type of gong can be heard right at the center of the earth. *CNN* is a blessing to everyone not only looking for information, but looking for a manner of addressing all issues of life as co-creators. Everybody is fully present, competent, professional and dedicated. Whoever recruits the people working at *CNN* is definitely a spiritual genius. Probably they have an entire team making such decisions. The synergy can be felt from the beginning to the end. *CNN* can serve as an excellent example for any working place.

While in our modern world employers use and abuse demographics as a source of discrimination, at *CNN* demographics are fully transcended. When we consider that for the majority of people work is a necessary evil needed for money to pay bills, it is phenomenal to deal with people who focus on self-fulfillment and a willingness to contribute all their talents and skills independent of other worldly considerations. I can imagine that there is place even for worldly considerations because they are a sign that no relevant aspect is denied. However, at *CNN* all priorities are set in the right perspective which again shows the application of the new energies of our time. I must add, I am a simple viewer of *CNN*, with the only difference being that I have access to energies. I do not know anybody at *CNN* and I do not plan to apply for a job there. I am making my statements only based on the energies I perceive.

Another institution deserving special mention in this context is the Royal Botanic Gardens at Kew. I had the privilege of watching the series made about their work on *BBC Prime* in the course of one year. Just as impressive, synergistic and spiritual as *CNN* and just as "groundedly intelligent". The attention, care, patience and meaning people put into their every decision manifests as a genuine work of art always passing the test of time! The Jewel-Island honoring the past, but still interacting with the present in a most spiritual way!

In case *CNN* and the Royal Botanic Gardens at Kew seem to be big exceptions, then I would like to add four other examples which I found out about by watching different documentaries at different times. All of them greatly touched me and moved me to tears due to their spiritual character and spiritual power. All of them are about anonymous people who are fully unaware of their profound effect on me. They might even ridicule me for my reaction to them, but I will take this risk upon myself without any reservation. In case some of them do ridicule me, it is only due to the fact that they have not yet realized that they are most deserving of the best in the world, instead of the usual pattern of the unwritten rule that they all belong to the least deserving in our world.

The first documentary was about the dabbawallas, the lunch-bringers, of Mumbai in India. These people also produce a gong right at the center of the earth every single day. I admire the dabbawallas for their "grounded intelligence" and their powerful expression of divine spark.

The next documentary was about the men working in the Singapore Harbor at the Tanjong Pagar Container Terminal, being in charge of the logistics of loading and unloading tons of products around the clock. I recommend that all the wannabe-heroes of the world have a closer look at these men and their contribution to our entire planet. It was remarkable for me to notice their spiritual characteristics which they seemed to take absolutely for granted.

My third special documentary was about the Hermitage in St. Petersburg and how the employees take care of the museum's cats. This was the documentary that made me feel that there are no more tears to cry. To see people who themselves have a very hard life appreciate universal life in the form of little kitties and their families was more than I expected in a world touched by greed, indifference and arrogance. The greatness of the human spirit was manifested in that documentary in the expression of Russian generosity and caring at its best!

The last documentary I would like to mention here was about Ecuador's banana plantation workers. I was deeply moved by the hard work so many people put into this type of labor, and every time I eat my organically grown banana from Ecuador, or any other Central or South American country, I think of the workers and their families in the most appreciative thoughts. These people also carry within a highly humble expression of divinity. I wonder if they are aware of how much joy they bring to others so far away from them. I hope Fair Trade as a new economic interaction truly serves the interests of the countries of origin. All the mentioned documentaries I watched either on the French-German *arte* or the German *3sat*.

From the global exposure of *CNN* to the wide spread reputation of the Royal Botanic Gardens at Kew, to the complete anonymity of Singapore, Mumbai, St. Petersburg and Ecuador, divinity is present everywhere at all times. I hope the few examples I mentioned are only a reflection of my tiny personal universe, in the hope that around our world every single day such examples can be found. Each one of us is a universe on its own. I assume that each one of them contains undiscovered treasures of divine potential. Maybe the conscious interaction with all the available treasures can help each one of us facilitate healing and the manifestation of creation as it was originally intended.

It is impossible to talk about "grounded intelligence" without mentioning education. THE way to bring "grounded intelligence" to the world is education. If even absolutist monarchs many centuries ago recognized the value of education and introduced it from their own devices to their entire populations, then it can only be our duty today to reinforce the spreading of education to every single human being and to base education on "grounded intelligence".

I feel I also benefited enormously from the American educational system based on "grounded intelligence" that I can only regard it as THE means for improving and healing our world and applying the new energies of our time in the most "grounded intelligent" way.

P.S: In case you ever wondered under what circumstances I said, "Not religious, spiritual!" – here it comes. I was at the hospital and the nurse who completed my medical file with me also asked me about my religious beliefs.

From the look on her face I knew that the answer, "Not religious, spiritual!" was unfamiliar to her, but I was going to make it worse for her by stating the following. "Even if I am not religious, if it represents any type of requirement I speak to representatives of all religions!"

The poor nurse was very insecure for a few seconds and had no idea what to answer. She was a very kind human being who realized within a split second that it was best not to comment.

There I was the personification of the opposite of religious prejudice. Apparently for the nurse as for most human beings, prejudice is not only more prevalent, but also easier to accept than lack thereof. She looked at me asking herself internally if there was any connection between the way I talked and the paralysis of all my extremities which brought me to the hospital in the first place.

"No need to put this crazy woman in a straightjacket because apparently she brought along her own internal one!" thought the nurse in reference to my medical condition. I was impressed by the nurse's willingness to be open and I wish I would have had the possibilities of sharing with her the entire information of my spirituality. She did very well in my eyes for the fact that I was a complete stranger to her, in an unusual physical state and talked like an extraterrestrial.

The End
(for now…)

ABOUT THE AUTHOR

This is soo funny!
Why?
Because I am all over my writing with bits and pieces of my bio, my philosophy, my interests, attitudes and values.

How about without being redundant here, you go to my website: http://cristi-anamontesanto.com

You could start by reading the Introductory Mini Short Story, a little piece that offers you a quick overview.
I wrote it for a competition. Needless to say, I won nothing. But I didn't write it at that time for winning. I did it because it was the right thing to do.
I knew I would need it one day. And here we are!
Every right thing has a purpose and a meaning independent of whether it ever wins us anything at all.

You could also have a look at the Free Reading Samples for a better idea of what my writing is about.

You might also find my Energetic Book Reviews interesting. Check them out!

If curious about the books I like to read, I recommend my GoodReads member page:
https://www.goodreads.com/user/show/69278527-cristi-ana-montesanto

I have many interests because, on the one side, I am open and, on the other side, I am curious.

Just like it is true for every human being, it is also true for me that I have many parts, facets and aspects.

In the final analysis, I am a synergistic whole with my own idiosyncrasies which include imperfections and deficits on the human level.

Independent of all my limitations, I am more than willing to contribute my talents to the improvement of the quality of life at both the individual and the collective levels.

I create my own rules, bend them if appropriate and even break them if necessary.

I always follow the flow of the energies. And my typical saying is: "Let me check the energies!"
Go figure!

Humorously but seriously,
Cristi-Ana

PUBLISHING HISTORY

PUBLISHED NEXT

Self-Awareness Calendar 2018
Version for Adults
Version for Children

IN PREPARATION FOR PUBLICATION

Memories from My Daughter's Childhood
A Message to Future Generations
A Trilogy

Website: https://cristi-anamontesanto.com/

10045156R00061

Printed in Germany
by Amazon Distribution
GmbH, Leipzig